COPING WITH TEACHERS

THE CONCISE

Coping with Teachers

PETER COREY

Illustrated by Martin Brown

Scholastic Children's Books,
Commonwealth House, 1-19 New Oxford Street,
London WC1A 1NU, UK
a division of Scholastic Ltd
London ~ New York ~ Toronto ~ Sydney ~ Auckland
Mexico City ~ New Delhi ~ Hong Kong

First published in the UK by Scholastic Ltd, 1991
Published in this version by Scholastic Ltd, 2000

Text copyright © Peter Corey, 1991
Illustrations copyright © Martin Brown, 1991

ISBN 0 439 99880 8

All rights reserved

Printed by Leo Paper Products, China

10 9 8 7 6 5 4 3 2 1

The right of Peter Corey and Martin Brown to be identified as the author and illustrators of this work respectively has been asserted by them in accordance with the Copyright, Designs and Patents Act, 1988.

This book is sold subject to the condition that it shall not, by way of trade or otherwise be lent, resold, hired out, or otherwise circulated without the publisher's prior consent in any form of binding or cover other than that in which it is published and without a similar condition, including this condition, being imposed upon the subsequent purchaser.

Sincere dedication

Since teachers have to put up with lack of respect, lack of chalk and lack of money, I'd like to dedicate this book to them. Most sincerely. And having done so, I can now get down to being really rude about them.

The root of the problem

Writing a book about teachers is not easy. For one thing, what if they catch me? Will I be made to stand in the corner? Kept in? Who knows! But let's start right at the beginning...

What is a teacher?

As always the best place to start when trying to answer a question as complex as "What is a teacher?" is the dictionary:

Teacher: n. Person who teaches, esp. in a school.

Brilliant!

Where do teachers come from?

Teachers start as children. They go to school, then university, then to teacher training camp. Then they go back to school. They bring everything they've learnt about the world to you, and you're expected to be grateful.

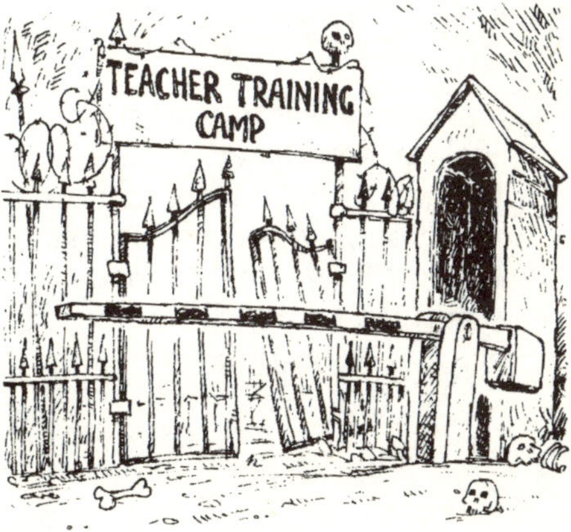
TEACHER TRAINING
CAMP

Teaching through the ages

It's probably worth pausing here to look at the bigger picture and try to understand how teaching has worked down the centuries and how it has been finely honed into the exquisite torture we know it to be today.

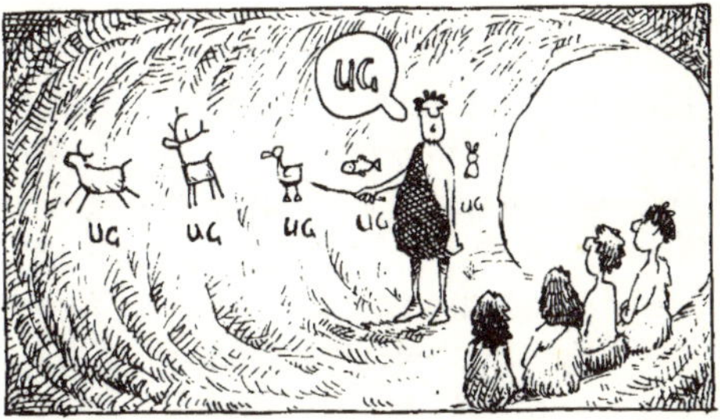
UG
UG
UG
UG
UG
UG

Ancient Greece

Ancient civilizations, like Greece, had philosophers who taught small groups of young men. Young women weren't allowed to join in because the ancient world didn't believe it was necessary to educate a woman. So who says teachers know best?

Roman around

The armies of Ancient Rome spread the concept of education as far afield as Britain, unfortunately. The Ancient Romans! Another great civilization! And where are they now? They can't even win the World Cup! More proof of the folly of education.

Shakespeare

Shakespeare was an educated man. He knew Greek and Latin. Mind you, he wasn't so hot on English or spelling, at least not if his plays are anything to go by. Shakespeare was a teacher. Did you know that? Probably explains why his plays are so difficult to follow.

ME THINKS THOU SHOULDST RECITE TO MINE EARS THE TIMES TABLE OF SEVEN..
WOT DID'E SAY?

Victorian England

Let's face it, many of our schools are still Victorian. Even some of the teachers are the same ones they had then. Schools were very strict: "Spare the rod and spoil the child." and schoolchildren were left quaking in their bare feet. The education of women was still not considered important.

The 20th Century

This is when teaching as we know it today came into force. Suddenly we were being forced to study such horrors as Latin, Sex Education and Woodwork. Girls were finally allowed to admit they had a brain and teachers were finally allowed to admit that they hadn't.

What makes them tick?

To understand what makes a teacher tick, you need to get behind that cloud of chalk dust and academic bluster and discover the person beneath the cardigan. A bit like ripping the mask off of the Phantom of the Opera and just as scary. Or alternatively, you can join MENSA...

MENSA

You might have heard of MENSA. Otherwise known as The Club For Brainy Folk. Apparently, a very large number of teachers belong to it. Yes, I can tell you're amazed. Teachers – intelligent? Well, let's see...

The metalwork teacher

Has a slightly greater than usual interest in metal. He's worryingly unconcerned about leaving his young students alone with a blowtorch, which makes you think that perhaps he's hoping for a nasty accident.

How to cope: Put your new skills to good use and make yourself a set of keys to the school!

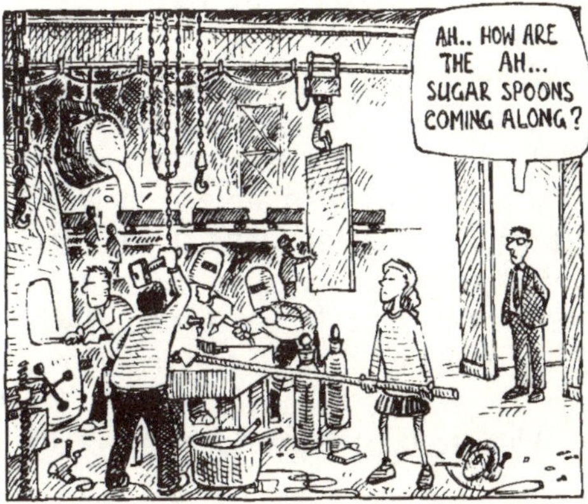
AH.. HOW ARE THE AH... SUGAR SPOONS COMING ALONG?

The woodwork teacher

Some woodwork teachers employ an interesting technique for shortening lengths of wood. They hit a student with a piece of wood, until it or the student snaps. Now that corporal punishment has been banned in schools, a sighting of this teacher type is very rare.

How to cope: Hide all the wood!

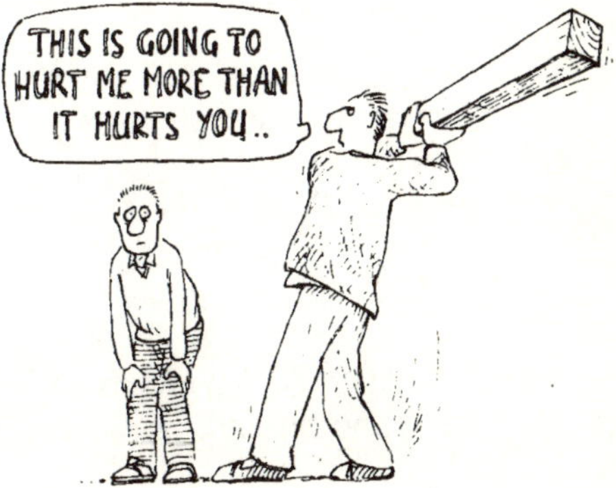
THIS IS GOING TO HURT ME MORE THAN IT HURTS YOU..

The geography teacher

He or she usually belongs to the rambling society and becomes a completely different person when exposed to fresh air. Often points to the sky saying things like, "Look! Cumulus nimbus!"

How to cope: Find a shrub to hide behind.

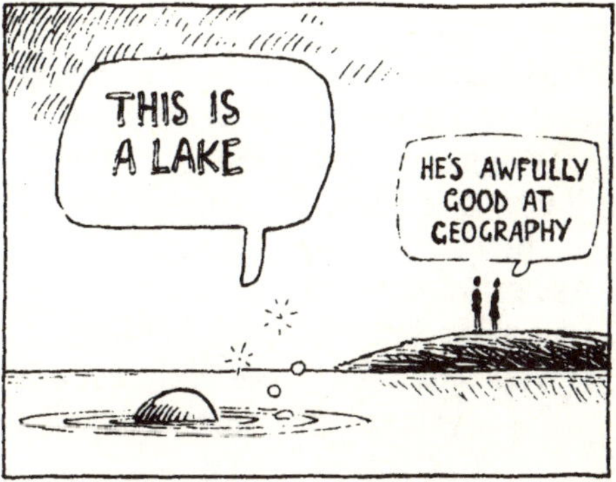
THIS IS A LAKE
HE'S AWFULLY GOOD AT GEOGRAPHY

Angry teacher

This teacher type is very common indeed. They're easy to spot because they're very loud. But, why are they shouting? Well, they've been told that it's an essential part of pupil control. If you make enough of an exhibition of yourself, the pupils will respect you for ever more.

How to cope: Earplugs.

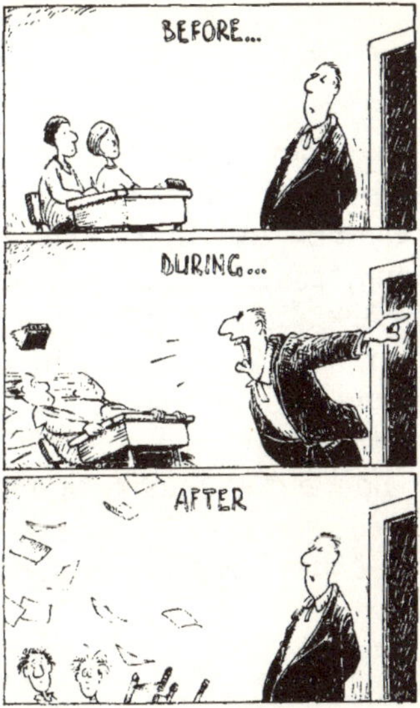
BEFORE...
DURING...
AFTER

Bald teacher

It's a fact of life that large numbers of teachers go bald. Mostly men, but there have been many cases of bald female teachers. Tension is known to be one of the major causes of hair loss and teachers can expect to spend a lot of time pulling their hair out in frustration.

How to cope: Buy them a hairpiece.

STUDENT TEACHER
FORM TEACHER
HEAD OF DEPARTMENT
HEAD TEACHER

Cowardly teacher

Found in cupboards. They occasionally venture out into the classroom, but only to tell the class that they are needed back in the cupboard. Their problem is fear of being asked to teach.

How to cope: Lock them in the cupboard.

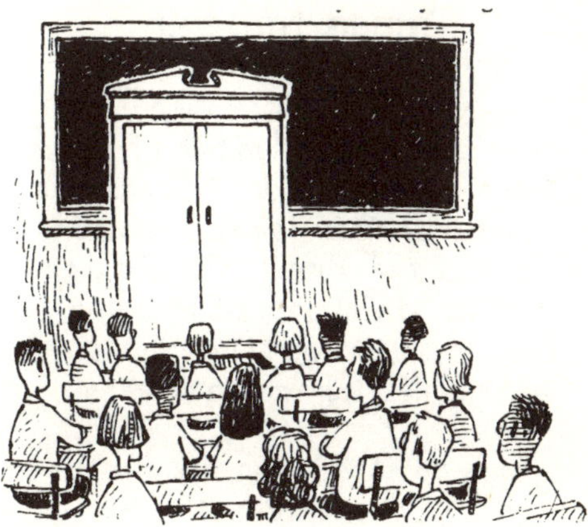

Dunce teacher

It may surprise you to learn that there are a large number of dunce teachers. So how do they become teachers? They joined the wrong queue at the Job Office and were offered the post of Head of English at a large comprehensive. It's called bureaucratic error.

How to cope: Stun them with your intellect!

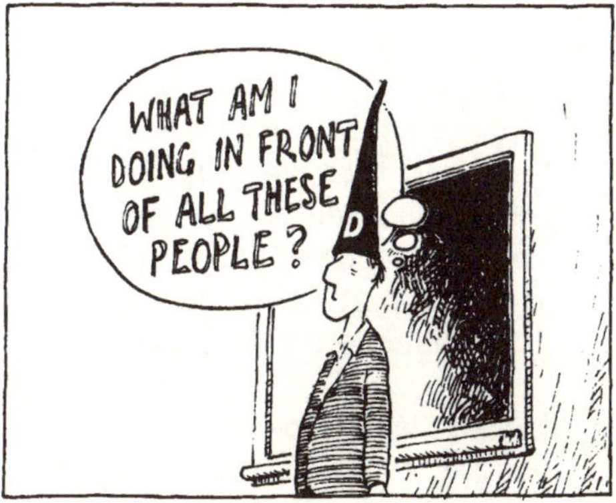
WHAT AM I DOING IN FRONT OF ALL THESE PEOPLE?
D

Educated teacher

In a way "educated" and "teacher" are almost contradictory terms. You don't need to be educated to teach. In fact, very often the highly educated person makes a very bad teacher, because they get frustrated by the lesser intelligence of their pupils.

How to cope: Look stupid – they won't want to have anything to do with you.

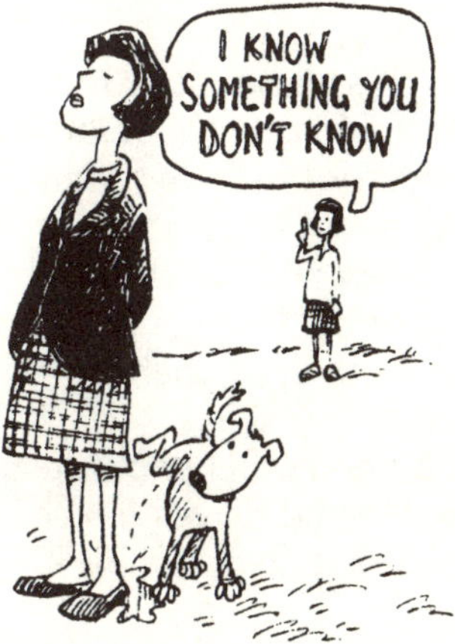
I KNOW SOMETHING YOU DON'T KNOW

Flash teacher

You must have seen them. Or heard their car. Or been dazzled by their jacket. Or fallen about laughing at them at the school disco. They want everyone to think they are a minor popstar, rather than a teacher.

How to cope: Burst out laughing whenever he drives his car into the school car park.

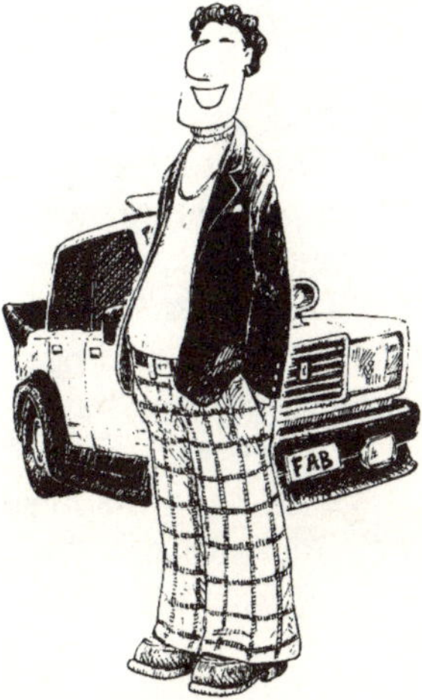
FAB

Genuine teacher

A rare breed, but they do exist, honestly. This teacher genuinely wants to pass on knowledge, despite their pupils' unwillingness to learn. They have a mission: to spread the word. And no one is going to stop them.

How to cope: A good disguise is the only way to avoid this teacher.

Harassed teacher

These teachers move from lesson to lesson like a typhoon, completely ignoring the school timetable which they're using to wedge up a corner of the desk. Don't be fooled, they're not absent-minded. They haven't got time to be.

How to cope: Avoid school corridors.

Interested teacher

There they are, happily teaching away, not causing any trouble or annoyance when suddenly they go: "Ah! That's interesting!", sit down and start reading. The class is then left to its own devices for the rest of the lesson.

How to cope: Hey! Don't complain!

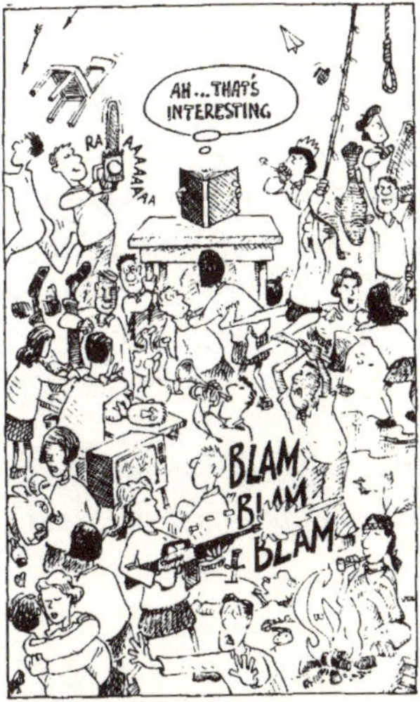
AH...THAT'S INTERESTING
RAAAAAAAAAA
BLAM
BLAM
BLAM

Judo teacher

Judo basically consists of someone thick as a brick trying to prove that they're also stronger than one. But what sort of people teach it? Usually, the type you'd least expect, like the softie English teacher who writes his own poetry.

How to cope: Avoid invitations to poetry appreciation lessons!

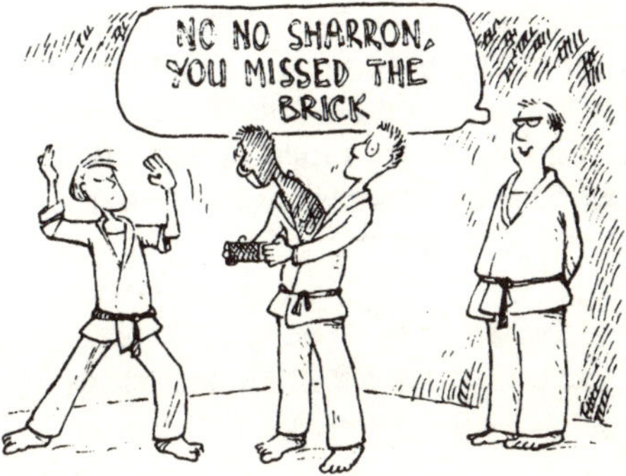
NO NO SHARRON, YOU MISSED THE BRICK

Kind teacher

My favourite type! Usually found in primary schools, they look like everybody's favourite aunt. Big, cuddly, with a large bust, woolly cardie and tweed skirt. And that's just the men! Only joking!

How to cope: There's no need to "cope". Just sit back and enjoy it!

Loud teacher

Don't confuse this type with the angry teacher. They're probably shouting because they're deaf. Unfortunately, they're often in charge of sex education, so prepare to be embarrassed if you're in their class.

How to cope: Try cotton wool balls in your ears, or a bag over your head.

Music(al) teacher

Found in the music room, tinkling on the piano during breaks. If they're not doing that, they're trying to persuade you to take up playing the triangle for the school concert.

How to cope: Buy a really old, obscure instrument and ask your teacher to show you how to play it.

Nasty teacher

These days it's very difficult to be a genuinely nasty teacher. I mean, physical violence is out. They can shout at you. But the best modern form of teacher attack is sarcasm. The trouble is, it loses its impact when you have to explain it.

How to cope: Pretend you don't understand sarcasm.

Optimistic teacher

If you catch your teacher smiling at you (unusual, I know), this might be a sign of an optimistic teacher trying to give you encouragement and support. Unfortunately, this special attention can make your life hell with your classmates.

How to cope: Blend in well with the background.

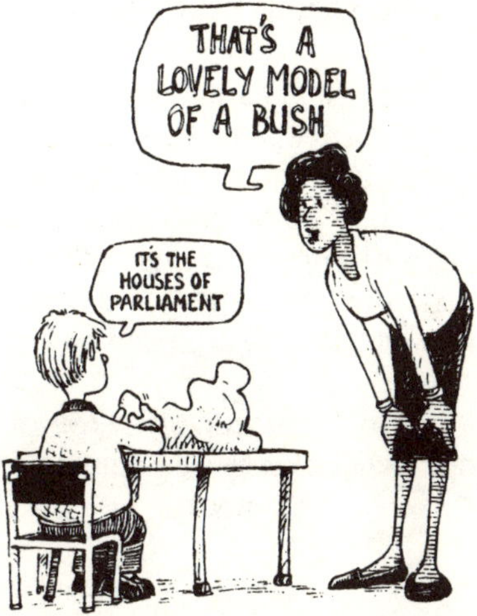
THAT'S A LOVELY MODEL OF A BUSH
IT'S THE HOUSES OF PARLIAMENT

Patient teacher

Teaching requires endless amounts of patience. Unlike the kind teacher, the patient teacher sighs a lot, just to let you know how patient they're being. Which basically gives the game away. They're not being patient at all.

How to cope: Run and hide if your teacher starts foaming at the mouth.

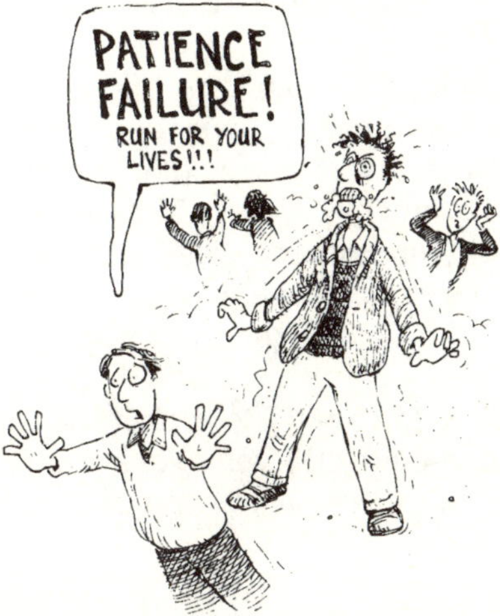
PATIENCE FAILURE!
RUN FOR YOUR LIVES!!!

Quiet teacher

"Look behind you!" as they say in the pantomimes. This teacher type can be lethal, especially if you've got a dicky ticker. They move quietly around the class, and appear over your shoulder when you're least expecting it.

How to cope: Short of having a radar built into your desk, there's not much you can do.

KEV, WATCH OUT.... WE'VE PICKED UP A TEACHER ON THE RADAR AND HE'S HEADING YOUR WAY..!.

Riding teacher

It's not every school that has a horse. If your school doesn't have a horse, but you do have a riding teacher, you may well find yourself astride your school chair repeating phrases like "Tally ho!" and "Giddeyup". You may feel rather foolish.

How to cope: Buy a hard hat and some furniture polish.

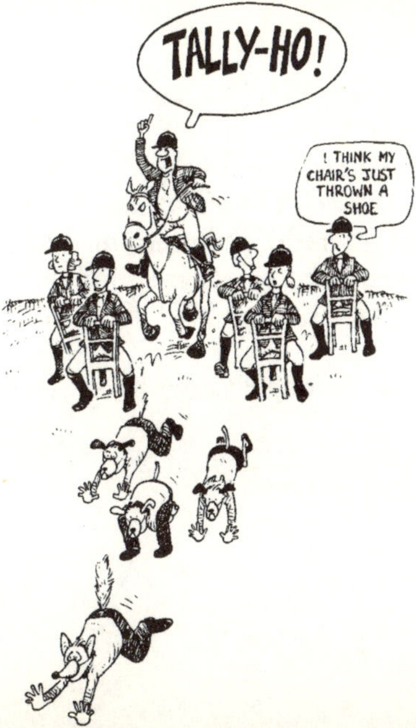
TALLY-HO!
I THINK MY CHAIR'S JUST THROWN A SHOE

Soporific teacher

It's quite common for teachers to fall asleep in the middle of a class. It's a condition known in medical circles as tiredness, and many teachers suffer from it.

How to cope: Leave them to it.

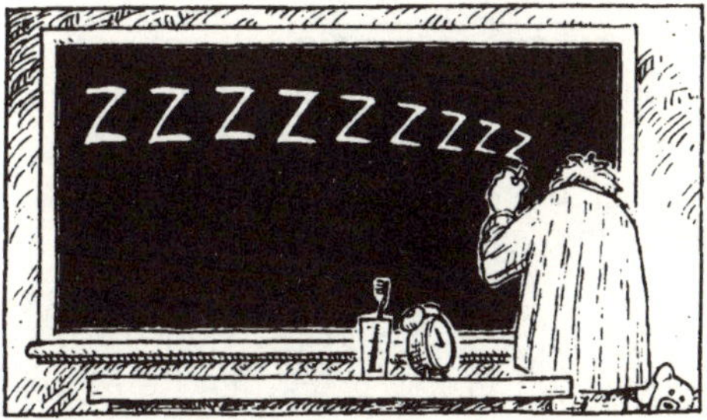
ZZZZZZZzzz

Tenacious teacher

This teacher type will get you educated whether you want it or not. They'll get those facts into your brain by any route possible. Up your nose if necessary.

How to cope: Don't let them catch your eye. It can work like hypnosis.

Useless teacher

This teacher is perfectly amenable but completely useless at their job. They usually look very confused and you can't help but feel sorry for them.

How to cope: Answer questions and help to improve their mind.

Varsity teacher

While the class stare vacantly at their books, Varsity stares longingly out of the window, drifting back to the dreaming spires of Oxford. They still wear their university scarf, even in the heat of summer.

How to cope: Knit them a new scarf!

Worried teacher

Look out for bitten nails and nervous perspiration. This type worries about everything – and it can be exhausting to watch.

How to cope: Slip a tranquilliser into their tea.

X-ray of teachers

Having managed to get a teacher on the X-ray table, I am able to go through some of the main identifying features of a teacher:

Brain: small. Hurts very easily.

Jaw: very flexible. Can go from shout to sneer in a hundredth of a second.

Heart: varies greatly in size, but can be practically non-existent.

Lungs: highly developed over years of classroom control.

Stomach: strong. Due to prolonged exposure to dinner duties and school plays.

Naughty bits: teachers don't have them, do they?

Y-bother teacher

You've probably heard this a million times: "I don't know why I bother." Many different types of teacher say this and throw their hands up in despair every five minutes.

How to cope: Work hard and smile. It's your only chance.

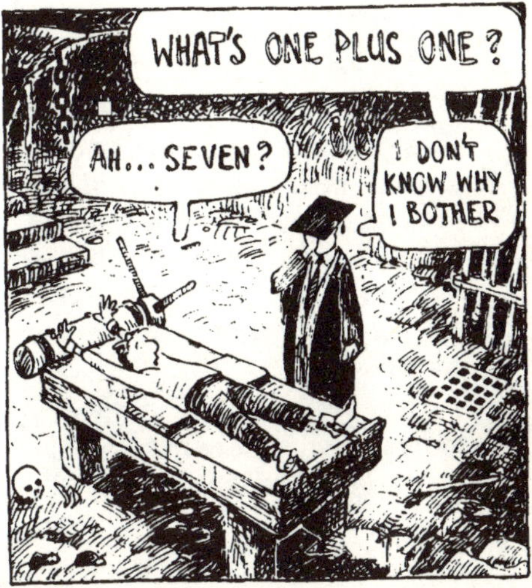
WHAT'S ONE PLUS ONE?
AH... SEVEN?
I DON'T KNOW WHY I BOTHER

Z-teacher
(head teacher)

The ultimate prize in some teachers' minds. A head teacher is someone who fills in when one of the proper teachers is ill and sets the class back by about three years.

How to cope: Not much to worry about, as you rarely meet your head teacher.

Is your teacher an alien?

Irrational behaviour and foaming at the mouth is normal practice for a teacher. So how do you tell if yours is an alien? You could take off their shoes to see if they've got webbed feet, but my advice is to leave well alone. After all, an alien might be preferable to a real, human teacher.

Where do teachers go on holiday?

Some go to the Cotswolds, some go to Butlins and others go to the Mediterranean. The main point to get across, is that even when you're on holiday you have to be careful, because you never know when a teacher is going to pop up.

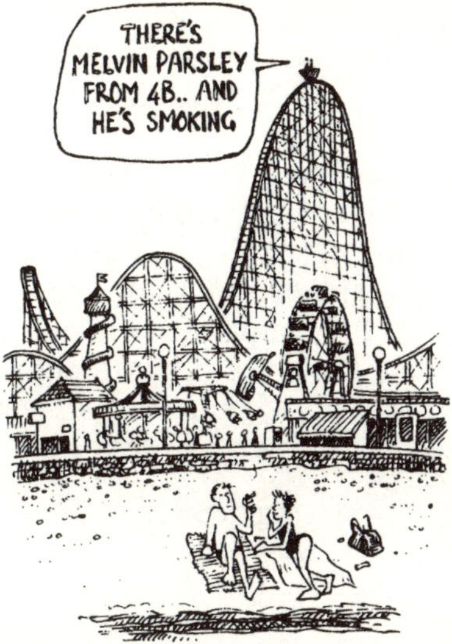
THERE'S MELVIN PARSLEY FROM 4B.. AND HE'S SMOKING

The secrets of the staffroom

Anyone who has managed to penetrate the Aladdin's cave that is the staffroom could tell you a thing or two. Well, they could except they've promised silence on pain of punishment by detention. Staffroom secrets must remain just that ... secret.

Algebra

You will realize, as you slide along the razor blade of life that much of what you pick up at school (in the way of knowledge, as opposed to a tropical disease) is of no use to you whatsoever. Take algebra, for example. I can assure you right now that there is no such thing as algebra in the real world.

Teacher qualifications

You need to be pretty bright to be a teacher. You also need to be able to grow a straggly moustache, wear a jacket with leather elbow patches and/or a nylon dress. But most important of all, you need some qualifications...

Passing exams

The way the system works is that basically, the more exams you pass, the better the choice of jobs available to you. In theory, at least. Turn over the page and find out about some of the jobs you might be able to do, if you pass your exams...

Number of exam passes

Ten or more

Eight to ten

Six to eight

Four to six

Two to four

One to two

Job opportunities

Lawyer, know-all,
teacher, astrophysicist

Captain of industry

Scientist, doctor

Vet, TV presenter

Politician, bestselling author,
dustman

Fireman, ballet dancer

School societies

Every school has a variety of societies or clubs that you can join: the school choir, the debating society or the theatre group. All of these activities are sold to you as fun, and all of them involve you being in the company of teachers for a lot longer than is reasonable.

If I was not a teacher...

It's worth pausing to consider what teachers would do if they weren't, erm, teaching. I mean, what the heck would they be any good at? Well, I've assessed the suitability of various jobs, and overleaf you'll find my conclusions:

Dustman

Let's start with the sort of job a teacher might be qualified to do. Early start in the morning. That wouldn't bother a teacher. It's a dirty job, but then so is teaching. But teachers would be for ever telling people off for not packing their rubbish neatly. They'd make them do it again.

GOOD WORK MR SAUNDERS, YOUR BIN LINER IS MUCH BETTER PACKED TODAY

Barrister

A teacher would probably enjoy going back to school to learn about the law. But they're not really suited. They'd be for ever shouting at the judge: "Don't interrupt while I'm talking! See me afterwards."

Accountant

Possibly the sort of job for a maths teacher, except that accounting is a creative art whereas maths is an exact science. Plus the fact that when you're doing someone's accounts, the answers aren't in the back of the book.

Chef

Could suit a home economics teacher. After all, it's only cooking. But there's one big difference. Customers in restaurants expect to like the meal. After all, they're paying for it. Whereas the food cooked in school by pupils is not expected to be fit for human consumption.

Could they cope?

I think these examples throw up the big difference between teachers and everyone else. They live in an institutionalized world where things are theoretical rather than practical, and have little or nothing to do with the real world. Let out, they simply couldn't cope with Real Life.

What teachers say

"That's lovely, dear!"

"Oh, hello!"

"Let me just go over that again."

"Can you all hold your books up please?"

What teachers mean

"What is it?"

"Oh, you're still with us, then?"

"I'm going to teach you this if it kills me!"

"I need to remind myself what I'm teaching."

Cars

The car a teacher drives into the school car park can tell you a lot about that particular teacher type. The student teacher drives a Mini, the hippy teacher drives a Beetle and the wise teacher walks to school. After all, who wants a bunch of kids taking the mickey out of your wheels every day?

Cardie

Another telling accessory often seen around the teacher is his or her cardie. Older male teachers tend to wear woollen ones with holes in the elbow. A female teacher often has a whole array of cardies in her wardrobe, and she's usually knitted them herself.

Discipline

Now, don't laugh, but a lot of teachers are very keen on discipline in the classroom. They're very keen on it, they just don't know how to do it. Instead, it falls to you to keep them in order and the best way of doing this is to question everything they do. The fact that you're even paying attention will unnerve them.

School breaks

These are the times of day when you are sent to stand outside come rain or shine, and teachers sneak off to the staffroom or - if it's lunchbreak - to the local pub for a swiftie. Lots of mischief is to be had during these breaks, so make the most of them.

Teacher training

This is one part of the school year, where the system actually works in your favour. Teachers are sent off for a reminder of what the heck it is they're meant to be doing, and you're sent home to make a nuisance of yourself. There's got to be a catch, surely...

Of course there is!

The catch is that your teacher comes back to school full of renewed vigour and enthusiasm and new ideas. You'll be expected to play guinea pig as they try teaching water sports in the paddling pool or physics by dangling you from the school roof.

PTAs

Otherwise known as Parent Teacher Associations. Basically, this is a group where your two worst enemies get together and compare notes on you. It's not nice and it's not clever and you'll be made to suffer. Just feel sorry for them – I mean, haven't they got anything better to do?

Form teacher

This is the teacher that takes the register and makes sure you've turned up for another day of hell. I think they're also meant to lend you help and support should you need it, but I've yet to see any evidence of that. Basically, these are the people who see you through the school year and laugh in your face as they do so.

Student teacher

This is a young adult who comes into your classroom to learn what it's really like to teach a load of monsters like you. The temptation is to make his or her life hell, but take a word of advice from me and leave them well alone. One day, it could be you stood in front of a roomful of brats and you'll wish you'd been a lot nicer.

Final bit

Naturally, a book like this can only scratch the surface of teachers (which is an OK thing to do, as long as you wash your hands thoroughly afterwards). But if you want the complete low-down on teachers and how to cope with them, you'll definitely need to read the full version of Coping With Teachers, available at the bargain price of £3.99 from all good bookshops (and a few bad ones!). It will be worth it!

Titles in the Coping With series:

School
Teachers
Parents
Friends
The Family
Pets
Boys/Girls
Love
Exams and tests
The 21st Century
Christmas
Cash